Apprehend

Apprehend

Elizabeth Robinson

Apogee Press · Fence Books · Saturnalia Books
2003

For Jonah, the messenger

Poems in this manuscript have been published in the following journals:

Conjunctions: Three Dragons, Hansel and Gretel
Fence: Whose Monster's Noise and Weather
Fourteen Hills: House
In Tense: Them (previously titled The Minpins)
Interim: Panoply
Ixnay: Passage (previously titled Regard)
Salzburg Poetry Review: La Colonia
Santa Monica City Poetry on the Buses: Field (previously titled Parable)
XCP: Cross Cultural Poetics: The Little Matchgirl

A slightly altered version of Topple was published in a chapbook length anthology, *Out of the Pit,* that was distributed to residents of New York City following the attack on the World Trade Center.

I wish to express my appreciation to the editors who have published my work. In addition, particular thanks go to Beth Anderson and Tiff Dressen for insight and response to this work, and to Ed Smallfield for his sustaining enthusiasm and support.

Book design by Philip Krayna Design, Berkeley, California.
www.pkdesign.net

ISBN 0-9713189-5-6. Library of Congress Catalog Card Number 2003101446.

Published by Apogee Press (www.apogeepress.com), Fence Books (www.fencebooks.com), and Saturnalia Books.

Printed in Canada by Westcan Printing Group.

Table of Contents

Introduction

The poems in *Apprehend,* as do all poems of consequence, resist both paraphrase and description. They are instruments of Elizabeth Robinson's elusive, haunting confrontations and minglings, her quixotic abrasions: trope rubs against statement, figure against logic, logic against figment. I am reminded, not a little, of Marianne Moore's dictum about poems being part imaginary toad and part real garden, of Barbara Guest's attenuated, observant mysteries, and of Marjorie Welish's deft evolutionary sequences. These are distant familial resemblances.

Reading *Apprehend,* re-reading it, one wonders. It is a curious kind of wondering: sober, introverted, circling around and through the nature of inception. How does a poem get to be conceived in the mind of a poet? How does apprehension lead to comprehension through formal ingenuity and imaginative force? An old wonder, one that comes from time to time when the job of making new meanings gives evidence of itself; when the reader is swept to attention, wanting to follow the offered thread that the writer has cast. But in this case, the thread, the narrative, dissolves, morphs, disappears and reappears, so that the act of following becomes almost an act of faith. One leaps across. One stops for breath. One wonders. The how and the what of language, its means and materials, are in a radiant conjecture; the poem coming into being simultaneously with the possibilities of its not coming into being. A frail balance, as if each word were shy of its rescue.

We enter the poem, there is a journey ahead; we embark. But here, the direction of the poem and the direction of the language of the poem are nearly at odds, as if one were on a track or path that had a second, ghostly path, hovering above or below. The diction is simple; the address is direct, if often abbreviated; and yet we find ourselves inside of a baffled urgency, as if against a wind. Here, as example, is the beginning of "Passage":

> Something falls from the heavens, the sky, the cloudburst itself
> and falls
> and crimps, reconfigures.

This "something," the subject, reconfigures before it has an identity; it is, the poem goes on, "arbitrary," and has landed on a hat of a passerby as a label or name tag.

> The name of this person come unbidden
> to hobble free passage
> as in the case of the fairy tale hero
> who walked backward in good faith
> and stumbled on vermin,
> progress and fine form disfigured.

The reader, like the hero, is hobbled in her journey through the poem, anxious between the objects and their arbitrary signs, terrified to fall backwards, to stumble on, say, a rat. In "The Little Matchgirl," the heroine's fingers are "divorced from their hands." From this grotesque, the poem investigates the nature of wishes, articulation (in the senses of digital joint and of language), hunger and poverty, transparency and coherence. Here, as elsewhere, Robinson evokes the familiar to stun us into re-cognition; she invites us to be readers who are able to believe, as a child might believe a fairy tale, in language as act. Indeed, Robinson draws frequently on children's stories in this collection, but there is nothing childlike here. In "Hansel and Gretel," for example, hunger and direction are taken up within frames of repetition and recognition. The story we remember sits under the poem like an armature.

Robinson wants us to acknowledge the ways in which language constructs both the world and our responses to it. She wants us to apprehend and then to comprehend. This is a poetics asking us to fully acquiesce in the potentially dangerous wonders of language as it travels through its arbitrary names, inventing as it goes. These inventions act like charms, spells, fairy tales, in that Robinson is fully prepared to allow whatever objects she puts in motion to undergo sudden, irrevocable shifts. These shifts alter the topography of the poem in such a way as to animate all the pieces, the materials, in the poem:

> Here is a blanket
>
> the abandoned image of the domicile
> refuses to huddle behind.
>
> Sons and daughters of structure
> do fly
>
> away and up—
>
> and behind,
> question collapses into request,
>
> how to go in,
> repining,
> how to swaddle the image of survival—

be it nourished off its own pests,
a peripheral spectre,
roof rising again in feigned dark.

By now we are almost prepared for the suddenness with which the apparition, the image, the spectre, will collapse and we will be without a structure in which to survive: homeless, footloose, no more than a mote, without volition or intention, will or desire. We are no better than Chicken Little, trapped in the doom of (history's) repetitions.

Little chick is redundant with his own doom.

His bomb has fallen into his lap

and the rest is all gaps.

Why would the world

be disobedient

and the sky hunch

over with its sickening bravery.

But the bravery in this book is the opposite of sickening, and its disobedience is everywhere conditioned by a powerful subversion of our habits of mind, our expectations as readers, our lazy desire to be comforted by the familiar. These poems brilliantly reinvent the moral reckonings common to all fable. Elizabeth Robinson reminds us to wonder and, in wondering, to experience wonder as the fault line between how the world is and what we apprehend in and of it.

—Ann Lauterbach

Three Little

A chimney turns gravity to creature.
What were we when we laughed at the impact,
the overflow.

Who had invaded us.

An argument. How to implant, literally, weight in beauty.
When we received you, I explained, some one had been looking up.

History marks refusal more than submission.
But little did we submit. There is a phenomenon
called fire. Someone, that is, came in
to acquiesce.

Tomorrow we sweep out the cinders and the black clods of wood.
The door is still locked. Our secure house is more gesture than matter.

Were there three of us sheltering there.
That wind was relevant. We had a bellows.
The record would have shown we sought confusion.
So did we inhale.

Air in space denounces the witness. Should
abode succumb to warmth or food. Do not look on
or fall. Hear this breath.

"Let me in" is disclaimer. Or I'll huff
on your mirror, bore through a peephole.
One jumps from chimney to fire in order
to renounce smoke. The quick fuel of air
against limbs.

The arrival is something like naked.
All the excess tarnishes and flares.

We could not welcome you otherwise.

· One ·

Field

A certain person
dug not the jaw
but the image of the jaw
from sod.

A certain sower
buries jaw
with seed.

Now the jaw
returns to its creature
in conflagration.

And certitude of earth
misdirects
the limited climate:

mouths fall with
rain and embed images.

Whose Monster's Noise and Weather

From what language does this beast extend,
joints like bracken

that it
eats what it finds
in its nest, even

the amniotic,
the cliche.

The basis of its confidence.

In a world posited as graceful,
where light makes shape,
why be bilious?
This is a variant of birth.

Should shape ostend
what the creature asks
of itself

as language,
the rain's shape:
a harsh comb

in its feather and fur

as one thing is to denude
another in the certainty
of the weather's plummeting water.

The terms
interchange, or blur.

Creature *is* rain,
is a saline cloud

bare of covering
in the crowd of
amorphous sky.

What is ringing out.

Its nest in its mouth
blurted and cirrus

while other morphemes
cling like garments

on its oily and resistant
back.

The struggle is trying
to wake them up
—pealing—
the progeny that never
were

as malleable and naked,
as likely to make water

and oil mix
to corporeal
conclusion.

And on the uplift of
the wind

what suffices as
patois,

wrecking and
bellowing inside its
inclination for

timeliness of air, confounding
sticky gust.

There is sometimes
a doubling back

even inside rebellion.

That was a lexicon
inside which he gestured
or sheltered
or kicked down.

The bluster of the universe, if it were
a bell—
he ate the clapper and
vomited it up to great
effect.

Three Dragons

AMPHISBAENA

How could you know yourself without your
mirrored voice,
your snarled hair,
your nose congested with smoke and mucous?

You are too world-weary to take the bait,
wheel-faced,
rolling aimlessly.

Down a feigned road
and up a red carpet

you strew: stumbling pebbles are
the issue of your glance.

And now, said the teacher, who will study the circle?
Who understands that it is

a study in contrast:
the most fierce and the least fierce?

And a student responds in the dark,
drawing hoops on his slate, on her slate.

The betrothed casts off the ring
and runs hurriedly to watch it

fall through the grating. The population
feared a creature said to

rise up

from the sewer. And so it goes,

the monster with its winning ways—

who is most diligent does not

pass the test
but wins it.

This is the charm that unravels the ring
and weaves the wreath.

Something smells amiss
and seductive:

the pupil

as suggestive.

The eye teaches

endlessness
in the shape of the curve.

Hush, the monster says,

in the fomenting dim,
in its rotation.

Hush the orbit.

How the betrothed studies deftness,

and who is it fetches the ring

by habitations of the sewer.

FIREDRAKE

i.

You are made in anti-alphabetical order.
Verbs, always in the accusative,
are vanquished by the genitive.
You will be buried in a cemetery with
circular walls.
But since death is unreliable,
you will repine—
the holiness of the site
is not sanctuary. A little kindling
breathes back at your fire. The vernacular
is, finally, a disappointment.

ii.
Now I was your lover
but so discreet,
you hardly knew what you did.
I took the thick rind off the fruit and to
your tender fangs. Where the fulcrum
of a myth is translation, firebreathing is not
just magic, it is strictly a set of rules. Orchards are
made of trunks. And the expenditure of branches—
and the artifactual arrival of fruit—

iii.
One day, you will be found
dead, and again not, and
in distress. Red
skin molting. Decoy.
Treasure. Those words most
besotted with you
are not those which are most loyal.

iv.

The dictionary I have in my hand
says that death and burial
are the same in meaning. I have not obscured
my relation to you as lover
sans beloved. No pages
torn from books. Sheer, with the minute print
of the bible. They came, and they were heroes,
and they tore away branches all oblivious to
fruit. They saw us light this up with sulfur—
and make pulp and mill the paper of secreted
documentary.

v.

Now a maiden loves a dragon,
and the dragon might
come upon a quality
of moral rightness and adopt it. The dragon
might be of surpassing beauty, of
indeterminate gender, might have
precise appetites. Circular wall. The dragon
reads on the throat of the maiden words
she cannot view herself. There are rules here,
you understand, that will not err
and cannot forgive.

WYVERN

Your claim
slips. Say it goes from wolf
to viper. It goes from arrow
to target. The scale of such things,
large as it is, transposes like plaques
that coat a threatened girth.

So now for you. Along comes the opponent,
not conversant with the lingo of the blur.
He strides into the barrow and laughs
to hear the bray of a donkey.

But you do not bray, you hiss. How
could an ear be so leaden. Ignorance unmade
as resource. Good will fornicates heartlessly
with offense.

You seal up the barrow.
You lick the seam of time. He may age,
you will grow ruddy
in the close air. Nevertheless,
the great hall of this passage
jeers in all blindness of your presence,
curving with satisfactions
and eternity.

Where presently
two unnameable creatures
are found conjoined in haunch and
gut, hands at pivot of clock
purely, and truceless.

· Two ·

Asea

Distant, a spire of the boat's temple
is visible

above the blanched timbers. Reconstituting
the floor of this coastal wood.

The sighted consume their tongues.

This is God as ass,
braying into our tears.

This is a saddle on the anchor, set sail
against tinny construals.

How we are moved toward battle and warped glass,
but moved by

our Lady, the ship, who prefers delicacy.
In whose arms once we scented

"north" and a "north"

we couldn't discern anyway,
concerned as we'd been for the knots adrift

in the tether.

The Book of Apprehension

Aside:

now I speak for myself
and say,
"Put those in the chase
into their right places."

It's my creator who
follows most furiously
and least well.

Who knows better my scent.
The elements of my making.

But no one can plumb what I pursue.

Any race run
can be run again
to losses
and gains.

The aspirant
runs past

to place one immobile object
in relation to another.

And he hopes that the relation
will endure.

His legs are brown,
his arms are brown.
His beauty was vegetal
as it sped by.

His beauty sped by
and the clarity
of his body
amended what

relation.

His face is simple and fine.
He makes the onlookers hunger.

The mouth struggles
with its intention,

the way a runner looks
back over his shoulder.

"Kiss" shapes itself by gait
and speed,

baton interchangeable from
mouth to mouth.

What is bitter and what is
finally caught in the same sentence.

Prize, booty, bag.

If we permit him to go on
this way, the exact fact is:
the spoils.

The mouth opens.

Think of anything
that cannot move.

This is his circling
gesture, face; course

that hasn't its own
volition.

Inside him
as fast as you can.

Taunt is faster than chant.

One who has no lover.
One who collects objects
and calls them his "wake."

This is what lips, tongue imply.
What is sanctuary, what is the lure

but a snare.

The slow unfolding that covers
his haste.

Passage

Something falls from the heavens, the sky, the cloudburst itself
and falls
and crimps, reconfigures.

It lands on the hat
of a passerby, a label:
a name tag.

Arbitrary like all the designations
that are received from above
or elsewhere.

The name of this person comes unbidden
to hobble free passage

as in the case of the fairy tale hero
who walked backward in good faith

and stumbled on vermin,

progress and fine form disfigured.

No one recalled his given, the name a lover
once whispered in his ear.

He was purchased as an object:
all progress is sacrifice.

What stranger tries gamely to greet him as familiar.

Though little do the sleepers know it
—those skeptical parents of life—

—forsakers of recognition—

this person stands on solid ground, but walks as if
on a tightrope.

Why is balance like the name tag, teetering, thready,

intent on sticking to its apparition?

Hunchback or prince
juggles appellation

while a child nearby earnestly explains

that in dreams the fall is exciting
and does not result in injury.

Child in the deserted promenade—

away, the benighted pedestrian:

to drop the juggled balls
is to make a decision from on high,

and the impact of the discarded balls
on the ground laminates identity

further.

A smart child,

he insists: but that person has disappeared.

And who walks on, shrugging,
good-bye to the invisible,
its spell broken

inside the transformations of mobility—
handsome and still hunchbacked.

Smart,
wise with gravity,
sincerely absent, extended like an old friend's hand.

So perturbs what should have ended already.

Things sent down seep
from one conclusion to the next.

A purgatory or so lower,
another child

looks up, goggling at the supposed sky.

A bird swoops down, maternal,
and plants a worm in her mouth.

In the world above, he offends his hosts by spitting in disgust.

Why he recedes through the membranous floor
that the other child pokes through,

because salvation is simply an exchange of names.

Treasure Chest

i.
Surprisingly, it is
small

and rather like food,
perishable.

A small thing
fits into a small hand,
clutched.

The precious,
in slant rhyme,

loses balance:

I find treasure

overturned on the kitchen floor;
at least a floor

to whelm the discarded
precarious.

At least the implication
of appetite.

ii.
The seeker
then boards a boat.

No floor underfoot.

Jewels-in-pocket
accompany that one

who wants
treasure,

the nature of treasure

being to appear transparent
as it reflects.

Treasure as seasick:
proper imbalance is
built into the journey.

Medicaments shine
in the pocket.

iii.
And come home again,
empty of pocket,

but finger full.
Anti-quest,

the hero wants only
to throw these findings

into a saucepan, the truest

nature of treasure

is modesty. Cook
the golden fish

in a familiar pot.
All that is precious

being so portable
as to be weighed

on one side or the other.

· Three ·

Formula

The idea is that you would dissolve yourself into water
          until the solution is cloudy and has

cleansing properties. Instead, you go away
          entirely. The water is left behind.

The water lacks churn, is unable to evaporate,
          tastes wrong.

Stymying the chemist: how to make water out of
          departure? How to make the water melt,

thinning the air? Froth, lather. That helplessness
          that comes of wanting to touch mutability.

It is a stubborn entity. It refuses to evaporate.
          It brings gifts of otherwise conforming

to the rules of the medium. You offer from yourself
          a house of water, but you are gone.

A property reclaimed at a distance. You would
          deliquesce, only after you leave. You wipe

away a certain soil only by staying,
          contrary. Wet footprints. You see a pattern

that reverts back to intention. Impracticable
          present.

As if to present oneself were an act of intent, a chamber
          of weightlessness. Not to float but to

remain there always, bidden by distance
          the solution in a thirsty knot bequeaths.

Them

The wind knocks a concise nest
from the top of a tree.
Yet it's not a nest,
it's a house
and it lands
on a plain.

The contents of the house,
a woman:
she soberly traces a cross
over her breast, and
a man:
he has a message pinned
to his shirt,
too small to read from here.

She will keep her promises.

He will hurtle

the pin which affixes him

to his message.

Up all night, the house
is watching them.
One could feel at its base,
like the nape of the neck,
what it was thinking.

Or
instead,
the woman traced
a cross on the paper
then the man
released it

and where it landed,
treasure.

Where it blew:
a map on a map

and the couple sleeps safe
in this house.

In what's underneath shelter
they talk,
and in speech, a tree,

bowed down from.

Now who is
the couple,
rocking back on their heels

hurt by the everyday
volume of speech.

That the landscape could be so much
smaller than the house,

the only house—

she in an apron
and he in breeches—
covering their ears.

A comical seriousness,
the house at its duty
lowers the tone

of the indolent wind
which protects by its
duck and cover.

The house sits astride the couple,
marking x-the-spot, pinned and mimicking

to the lost message shushing the plain.

House

Ladybug, ladybug, fly away home...

Figment or insect
serves up admonition—

and every motion
is a copy, a lie

out of whole cloth,

burning. Leaves curl
imitatively

in flame.

Reference
confounded with rhyme:

the chimney as an organ
of meditation, it turns back

on itself, thought matched to thought
like a pair of shoes.

They stomp,
choke out

that blemish, the fireplace.

A dwelling, continuous, of smoke
saunters down a falsified road.

Evacuees are progeny,
wrapped in replicative ash.

Here is a blanket

the abandoned image of the domicile
refuses to huddle behind.

Sons and daughters of structure
do fly

away and up—

and behind,
question collapses into request,

how to go in,
repining,
how to swaddle the image of survival—

be it nourished off its own pests,
a peripheral spectre,

roof rising again in feigned dark.

Topple

In seven minutes the sky will fall.

In this minimal world,

the week is a chick

curled up,

and blinking at the sky

who so obliges, its own curl

into downturn.

Foolproof to predict the event

as it occurs:

ergo rain's blot is prediction

and the frightened chick

runs around the maze,

line by line, inside each cloud

sniffing the future.

Now that the sky has fallen,

its pieces harden

and those

who try to tack it up

frustrate the shape it had wished

to be by the one-too-many fingers

of their own obdurate balance.

Little chick is redundant with his own doom.

His bomb has fallen into his lap

and the rest is all gaps.

Why would the world

be disobedient

and the sky hunch

over with its sickening bravery.

Not the sense

of loss, but actual lostness

should not commit to response

to the feather falling from dust

until the sky merges

again with itself.

The gravity of itself

is what it regrets.

· Four ·

Panoply

You can sit here:
there are three bowls from which to select.
There are three stairs,
three chairs, three glowing tresses
draped across the beds

while the lock turns the key
aside. Here, you may rise
to keen the terms of escape.
The window defines the house
but spurns its duty to view.

The stability of the set, its contents:
too hot, too cold, just right. And looking in
at its array, three verbs make as if to rise or recline

out of sight
in the brackets of that
set in the woods, that
house, that flight.

The Little Matchgirl

The fingers were divorced from the hands.
Now there is a glowing
around the numbness of the mouth,

and that
light-ridden
painlessness is
the hand.

Hold the flame
up to the detached fingers.

Sensation as pentimento, overlap.

(Revoke her poverty.)

Wish is a form of overlap,
of articulation:

to unite by a joint or joints.

Or the smooth-jointedness
of x-ray vision:

looks through walls
from the empty belly
to the feast.

While this wan fist

has no knuckles
to penetrate
coherence.

Would a second wish
lay on the bed of the first
as if to put words to,
or interpolate a blanket.

Leaf back through definition
and you will find her
lying there,

betrayed by those ghostly fingers
who point,

and ignited on the flint
of the abandoned
street.

And distinctly
unwarm in the gesture.

Perhaps you are happy with yourself
because you are familiar with a story
like this, and you experience the wall, too, as transparent.

Do you know the segments, the succession?
Perhaps you experience the bare palm as an embarrassment—

the disjointure,
the disarticulation
are not a muteness.

Shame on the fingertips:
matchtips
strewn with sulfur and phosphorous
do not remediate a bitter cold.

(You have been eavesdropped upon
when the image fell from the lips.)

She saw as a physical part of her heart
the pulse of some extremity.

Transparent or amputated:
admitting the passage of light through interstices.

What third vision spies
back upon her
hinges upon

the ability to move

while the false narrative of her
contentment is frozen.

The wicks of the fingers
one from another so far.

Hansel and Gretel

Trail strewn with neon crumbs.
If one were to lay out such alternatives:
the sower's hand was deft
and the specks tossed and levitated on air.
If not that one,
                    then this—
properly halting—
if not geography, then ethics.
Abandonment
chastens the floating morsels to the level of the mouth.

Benign path and
trees being what they are,
wooden.
No apparent peril
and desertion—
always coming back
to a mouth.
The wicked stepmother
is merely hungry and absentminded.
Thatches fall from the roof of the house
and her vague hair.

Their father and his yawn.

If there is no evil one,
then there's merely philosophy
and N.'s speculation about endless
repetition
is correct.
The candy house is intricately patterned.

The witch herself wears stripes,
marking her as a pariah.
How she happened to know
that there are options even in repetition:
starvation breeds resourcefulness.

Yes, she paints one line atop another
until the stripe itself acquires dimension
and curls like a tongue
from the limits of two dimensionality.

She paints one line atop another on her naked form
to mimic the grain of a tree.
Those who are wooden and those who are not.
How she happened to know
the pattern of errant wanderers

on her tongue
and its limits.

Brother and sister
share a tentative kiss.
Not of passion,
but of its many alternatives
they choose security.
Hunger and its relation to resource.
The door to the confectionery
shelters.

Now side by side they lay
innocent of each other,
but parallel as their bodies
line the boundaries
of a path.

Not to obstruct but to fill,
so that when satisfaction
is not complete,
they serve other purposes
and lead onward.

Simplicity plies this version of a trail
with tidy piles of white
crumbs and pebbles.
But as the crow flies,
they remain completely entangled.

The girl curls up
and the boy stretches into such posture
that, seen from above,
he forms the profile of the witch's face.

But everybody knows the general outlines of inevitability.

The witch, stripes gone askew,
is crosshatched.

An old story, told yet again,
is subject to certain deformations.

Two children, mad with hunger,
impose themselves on a gentle old crone.
They hustle her into her house,
and finding her larder bare,
they attack the house itself and try to consume it.

Some ideas are planted insidiously in the tree's pattern,
rippling through its grain and gnarling by design.

You have grown weary
of this story's slow progress.

You look at a fantastical candy house,
its reflection warped and wavering.
You turn from its reflection in
an unnamed body of water.
You turn, go, and sink your teeth in.

While they
retrace their steps
by walking backwards—

in the meantime,
all destinations
having been razed.

The marzipan roof
of the forest, the
chocolate cloud, the
way the world accommodates
their misadventure, the embrace of

the crisp pastry. The relation
resumed to direction, to
parent, to knees as they
bow to the slick candy
surface of the way. And

their young backs always to
the various endpoints
from which they came.

What is most important is that
they learn the skills of recognition.
I'll swear by all my witchery
that this is what any parent
most wishes for her children.

You, Reader, come closer
and extend your fingers
through the bars of the cage

so I can feel their pleasing tenderness:
be our mirror.

For you
are neither boy nor girl
but the certain

unity of the sweet abode—
a spun sugar house
adorned all over with
white pebbles and bread crumbs.

We do not want you to find your way.
We so want for you

to see the mirror.

To deceive us hardily
and to roll
from the edges of the path
against parallel,

connecting, central and skew
and endlessly
thumping shins against shins,
the brush of hand on hair,
the bodies' alternative

to direction is

recognition and ceaselessness.

La Colonia

You are offered no direction,
but a velvet jewelry box,
empty of contents, gives
legend to the neighborhood map.
Dark outside. Sparks in the opal
make morning
come. Half-domesticated
creature gnaws at the border
of the precious, until you change
its order
and a semi-domestic hedge
adopts the traits of a dear friend
gone around a corner
into a park, just a few minutes
before dawn.

A childhood memory:
the lawn's damp on the ankles
murmurs that "this place, here"
is no longer a reliable utterance.
This place, here,
around the corner of the gate
like an interruption of the smooth
inside the jagged.
There is always a park-like plane
across which one struggles to keep up.

But you are lagging,
preoccupied with the memory of a friend,
who holds you with a literal hand,
is it cupping or restraining?
The glint
a lesser jewel has,
and all the subsequent
iterations
of landscape or affinity.
That's the way the gate
keeps apace of the park
in the dim morning's
greater topography.

OTHER POETRY TITLES FROM APOGEE PRESS

Rules of the House
by **Tsering Wangmo Dhompa**

"A lovely explication of 'dharma'—things as they are and how precious they are." —Anne Waldman

fine
by **Stephanie Marlis**

"An etymology of our sexual and physical lives, our unknown lives, our daily lives." —Edward Kleinschmidt Mayes

Speed of Life
by **Edward Kleinschmidt Mayes**

"These poems are at the harsh center of things." —Eavan Boland

Human Forest
by **Denise Newman**

"Like imbibing a divine elixir, making one realize how thirsty one has been all this time." —Gillian Conoley

The Pleasures of C
by **Edward Smallfield**

"These are poems of thrilling uneasiness and probing reward." —Kathleen Fraser

Oh
by **Cole Swensen**

"Oh is opera cool." —Marjorie Perloff

placing the accents
by **Truong Tran**

"A voluptuary of the difficult real. To be entered, and entered. Gratefully." —Kathleen Fraser

dust and conscience
by **Truong Tran**

"Something extremely important is going on, something wonderful." —Lyn Hejinian

OTHER POETRY TITLES FROM FENCE BOOKS

Nota
Martin Corless-Smith

Father of Noise
Anthony McCann

The Real Moon of Poetry and Other Poems
Tina Brown Celona
2002 alberta prize

The Red Bird
Joyelle McSweeney
2002 fence modern poets series

Can You Relax in My House
Michael Earl Craig

Zirconia
Chelsey Minnis
2001 alberta prize

Miss America
Catherine Wagner

FENCEbooks

Fence was launched in the spring of 1998. A biannual journal of poetry, fiction, art and criticism, Fence has a mission to publish challenging writing distinguished by idiosyncrasy and intelligence rather than by allegiance with camps, schools, or cliques. Fence has published works by some of the most esteemed contemporary writers as well as excellent writing by the completely unknown.

Fence Books is an extension of that mission: with our books we provide expanded exposure to poets and writers whose work is excellent, challenging, and truly original. The Alberta Prize is an annual series administered by Fence Books in collaboration with the Alberta duPont Bonsal Foundation. The Alberta Prize offers publication of a first or second book of poems by a woman, as well as a five thousand dollar cash prize.

Our second prize series is the Fence Modern Poets Series. This contest is open to poets of either gender and at any stage in their career, be it a first book or fifth, and offers a one thousand dollar cash prize in addition to book publication.

For more information about either prize, visit us online at www.fencebooks.com, or send an SASE to Fence Books/[Name of Prize], 14 Fifth Avenue, #1A, New York, NY 10011.

For more about Fence, visit www.fencemag.com.